Polar bears

by Helen Orme

Copyright © ticktock Entertainment Ltd 2006
First published in Great Britain in 2006 by ticktock Media Ltd.,
Unit 2, Orchard Business Centre, North Farm Road,
Tunbridge Wells, Kent, TN2 3XF
ISBN 1 86007 965 2 pbk
Printed in China
A CIP catalogue record for this book is available from the British Library.

We would like to thank our consultant Downs Matthews,
Director Emeritus, Polar Bears International

Picture credits
t=top, b=bottom, c=centre, l-left, r=right
Alamy: OFC, 6-7, 8-9, 10-11, 13, 14-15, 16-17, 18t, 19, 20, 22-23, 25, 27t, 28b.
Corbis: 4-5, 12, 18b, 21, 27b, 29b, 31, 32.
Every effort has been made to trace the copyright holders, and we apologise in advance for any unintentional omissions.
We would be pleased to insert the appropriate acknowledgements in any subsequent edition of this publication.

CONTENTS

Words that appear **in bold** are explained in the glossary.

LIFE IN THE ARCTIC

The Arctic is the **habitat** of the world's biggest land **predator** – the polar bear.

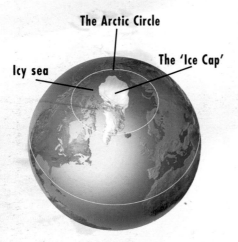

The Arctic Circle

The 'Ice Cap'

Icy sea

In the Arctic Circle a large area of the sea is frozen all the year round. This is called the 'Ice Cap'. In winter, the sea around the Ice Cap freezes, too.

Polar bears spend the autumn, winter and spring hunting on the frozen sea.

MOTHERS AND CUBS

In early winter, a female polar bear will build a den by digging into a snow bank. Her cubs will be born here, two metres under the surface.

The den is about a metre high and two metres long.

The mother bear will make a narrow air hole into the den and the family will live here right through the winter.

BABY FOOD FACT

In the den the cubs will feed on their mother's milk, but the mother only has her body fat to live on.

LEAVING THE DEN

In early April the family will leave the den.

The mother has had nothing to eat for months, and she must hunt for food. If she starves, her family cannot survive.

Hungry predators, such as wolves and adult male polar bears, will be on the look-out for bear cubs to eat. The mother must guard the cubs carefully.

Polar bear families stay close to the den entrance for the first two weeks.

A LIFE IN THE SEA

Polar bears are strong swimmers. They spend a lot of time in the sea swimming from **ice floe** *to ice floe, hunting for seals.*

They use their **webbed feet** as paddles and their thick, oily fur keeps them warm in the freezing water.

Polar bear cubs quickly learn to swim. If they become tired, they can travel through the water on their mother's back.

FINDING FOOD

The polar bear's main food is seals.

Polar bears will wait at holes in the ice that seals use when they come up to breathe. When a seal appears, the polar bear will pounce and kill the seal with a blow from its paw.

Polar bears spend over half of their time hunting. Even so, they may only catch a seal once every four to five days.

HELPING THE NEIGHBOURS

Adult polar bears mainly eat seal **blubber**. They leave the meat. This is eaten by young bears and other animals such as Arctic foxes.

HUNTING POLAR BEARS

The **Inuit people** of northern Canada have always hunted polar bears for their meat and fur.

When hunters from other parts of the world started to come to the Arctic to hunt polar bears for sport, too many bears were killed. Laws were passed to limit the hunting.

Now only a few bears can be hunted each year by the Inuit people, and all hunters need a licence.

A NEW DANGER

*Now there is a new danger for polar bears – **global warming**.*

Polar bears need the floating sea ice to hunt for seals. Global warming means that the sea ice is melting earlier and freezing much later in the year. If there is no ice in the spring and autumn, polar bears have less time to hunt.

The ice-free sea also makes it difficult for polar bears to travel. Bear cubs and young bears cannot swim the long distances between the ice floes.

COMING TO TOWN

Sometimes hungry polar bears will come into the towns of northern Canada looking for food.

Polar bears will not usually kill humans unless they are angry or frightened. But they can be dangerous, so people in the towns need to be protected.

Special hunters shoot the polar bears with a dart gun to send them to sleep. The bears can then be taken away to a safe place by helicopter.

This bear is searching for food on a rubbish dump.

STUDYING THE BEARS

Scientists don't just use dart guns to capture polar bears that come into towns.

Darting is an important way of finding out about the animals so that they can be helped.

When a polar bear has been put to sleep, scientists can weigh it. If finding food is getting more difficult, polar bears may be getting thinner. Regular weighing helps to keep a check on this.

KEEPING TRACK

Sometimes polar bears are fitted with radio collars. These collars send signals to a satellite so scientists can track the polar bears to see where they go to hunt.

A DIFFICULT FUTURE?

Life may be very difficult for polar bears in the future.

Global warming is damaging their habitat and making it hard for them to hunt.

Drilling for oil and mining is causing **pollution** and changing the **environment** where they live.

A lot is being done to save polar bears. Scientists now know a lot more about them, and fewer people are hunting them.

Polar bears can survive into the future – but they will need our help.

In this picture scientists are studying polar bears from a special bus. Some of the people are on a polar bear-watching holiday.

WHERE DO POLAR BEARS LIVE?

Polar bears live in the Arctic Circle at the very top of the Earth.

The colours on this map show what happens in the Arctic Circle throughout the year.

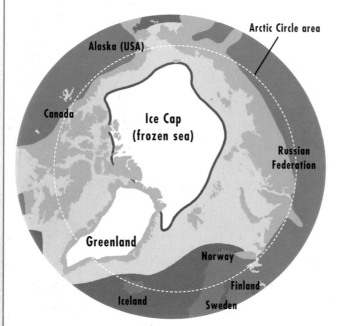

☐ Sea that is frozen all the year round.

Sea that freezes in winter and breaks up into drifting ice in summer.

Sea that does not freeze in the winter.

Tundra – land that is covered with ice and snow in winter. In summer, the snow melts.

• The Arctic Circle is full of life. The sea is full of fish, whales and seals. In summer, small, tough plants grow on the **tundra**.

Over 500 different types of plants grow in the Arctic Circle.

POLAR BEAR BODIES

Polar bears are the biggest, land-living predator on Earth.

• Polar bears have two layers of fur to keep them warm and dry.

• Polar Bears have small ears and noses, so that the animals lose as little heat as possible.

Male

Length: up to 3 m
Weight: up to 600 kg

• Polar bear paws measure about 30 centimetres across. They are webbed for swimming and have hair on the soles to grip the ice.

Female

Length: up to 2 m
Weight: up to 350 kg

POLAR BEAR FOOD

• The polar bear's most important food is the ringed seal. They will also hunt and eat small whales, dolphins and walruses.

• If meat is hard to find, polar bears will eat berries, grass and other plants.

• In winter, polar bears hunt seals on the frozen sea. In summer, they have to stay on land with very little to eat.

• Polar bears can smell food from 32 kilometres away!

ARCTIC FOOD WEB

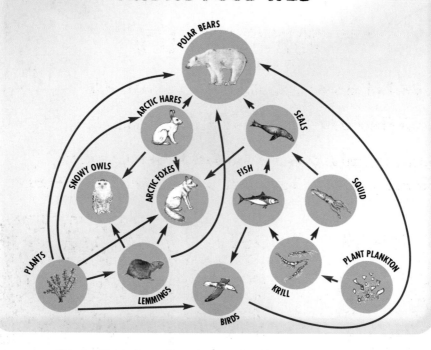

This food web shows how the animals and plants living in the Arctic Circle depend on each other for food – both on land and in the sea. The arrows in the web mean 'give food to'.

POLAR BEAR CUBS

• Polar bears mate in the spring.

• The cubs are born in a den during January and February.

• When they are born, cubs are only 30 centimetres long and weigh about 500 grams.

• Cubs stay in the den until they are about three months old.

Cubs stay with their mother and drink her milk for about three years.

POLAR BEAR LIFE

• Few polar bears live longer than 18 years in the wild.

• A polar bear can run at 40 km/h in short bursts.

• Polar bear bodies are so good at keeping warm, the bears sometimes get too hot. They cool off by swimming or eating snow.

A polar bear spreads his belly on the snow to keep cool.

HOW MANY POLAR BEARS?

*No one knows exactly how many polar bears there are.
The best guess is between 25,000 and 40,000.*

DANGERS TO POLAR BEARS

• Polar bears are protected by law in the Arctic Circle countries.
Inuit hunters are allowed to kill a small number of animals each year,
but **poaching** of polar bears is hard to control.

• People are trying to find oil, gas, diamonds and metals in the Arctic.
This could cause problems for the polar bears. Lots of extra people
in the area will disturb the animals.

• The mining and drilling could cause pollution, especially in the sea.

What will happen to the polar bears' habitat?

GLOBAL WARMING
THE BIGGEST THREAT TO POLAR BEARS

- *What is happening?*

The Arctic is warmer now than it has been for 400 years.

This means that the Arctic ice is beginning to melt. Scientists say that the Arctic Ocean might be ice free by the year 2080.

- *What is causing this?*

Most scientists now believe that the warming is caused by **greenhouse gases** trapping the Sun's heat in the **atmosphere**. The main reason why the amount of these gases is going up is because we are burning so much oil and coal.

- *Why will this affect polar bears?*

Polar bears need the sea to freeze so they can go hunting. If the ice melts, they will not be able to catch the seals which live out at sea.

HELP THE POLAR BEARS

• Find out about polar bears and other animals in danger. Do a project or a display at your school to tell other people about them.

• Join an organisation like the *World Wildlife Fund* or *Polar Bears International*. They need to raise money to pay for their **conservation** work. See the websites below for lots of fundraising ideas.

• Be a good conservationist. Save energy to cut down on global warming by turning off lights you don't need and walking or cycling to school instead of going by car. There are some good ideas to help you on the *Go Wild!* section of the *World Wildlife Fund* website.

**Visit these websites for more information
and to find out how you can
help to 'Save the polar bear'.**

Polar Bears International: www.polarbearsalive.org

World Wildlife Fund International: www.wwf.org.uk

Born Free Foundation: www.bornfree.org.uk

GLOSSARY

atmosphere A layer of gases that surrounds the Earth.

blubber A layer of fat around the body of animals such as seals, whales and polar bears.

conservation Taking care of the natural world.

environment The area where an animal or plant lives, and all the things, such as weather, that affect that place.

global warming The heating up of the Earth. It is caused by greenhouse gases trapping heat from the Sun in the Earth's atmosphere.

greenhouse gases The gases caused by burning oil and coal.

habitat The place that suits a particular animal or plant in the wild.

ice floe A floating sheet of ice.

Inuit people Native Americans who have lived in the Arctic for hundreds of years. They fish and hunt for seals and polar bears.

poaching Breaking the law by trapping or killing wild animals for food, or to sell.

pollution Oils, rubbish or chemicals that have escaped into the sea or air, or onto the land.

predator An animal that lives by hunting and eating other animals.

tundra Cold land that is always frozen under the surface and covered with snow in winter. When the snow melts in summer, the land is covered with low-growing plants.

webbed feet Animal feet with skin between the toes to help with swimming.

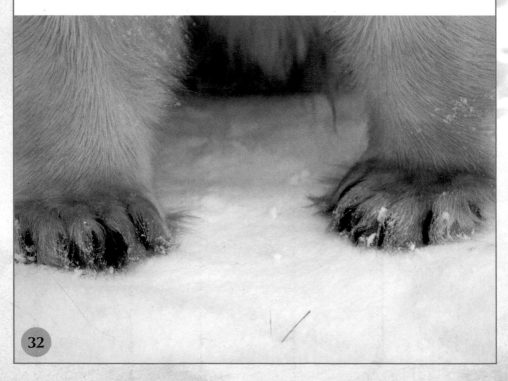